Local News

Local News

Glen Downie

Wolsak and Wynn

Cover image: Glen Downie
Layout and Design: Leigh Kotsilidis
Typeset in Bradley Hand ITC & Corbel

Canadian   Patrimoine
Heritage   canadien

The publisher gratefully acknowledges the support of the Canada
Council for the Arts, the Ontario Arts Council and the Canada Book Fund for their
financial assistance.

The author gratefully acknowledges the support of the Canada Council for the Arts.

Wolsak and Wynn Publishers Ltd.
#102–69 Hughson Street North
Hamilton, ON
Canada L8R 1G5

for my neighbours

Of all the works of man I like best
Those which have been used.
The copper pots with their dents and flattened edges
The knives and forks whose wooden handles
Have been worn away by many hands: such forms
Seem to me the noblest. So too the flagstones round old houses
Trodden by many feet, ground down
And with tufts of grass growing between them: these
Are happy works.

– Bertolt Brecht

Hope in gates, hope in spoons, hope in doors, hope in tables ...

– Gertrude Stein

Contents

HOUSE

HOUSE

The first house grew out of place, was of one nature with its element. So a house on red earth was itself red earth, formed by touching wet hands to the ground, then packing the mud into a greater and greater hill, then tunnelling a doorway, and, deeper inside, a space to sit by the fire. Within this hollow, a window was fashioned for vision and a breath of fresh air, and a hole in the roof for the exhalation of the spirit.

Thus did a dweller on red earth live *inside* the red earth. On grasslands, the house was a house of grass; where there were trees, the house was of trees. In lands where there was only snow, the house was a mound of snow. Everywhere the house and the earth were one substance. Everywhere the yielding earth puckered and folded its skin, stretching and expanding, such that what was called *house* was no house at all, but a gall on the body of the earth, an accommodation to a species of burrowing parasite.

PORCHES

Modern builders prefer blunt boxes that press us without ceremony nose-to-nose with the front door. The old way is slower, more patient, subtle. It suggests, even when it does not fulfill, a Southern gentility where couples sat of an evening on the royal dais above a tiny grass kingdom, watching the world stroll by, nodding beneficently to strangers, calling out to neighbours, issuing casual invitations to friends whose company might be welcome. Those called in this way might then stand, one foot on the step, before being asked to sit. And having porch-sat a while, if confidential matters were to be spoken, might then be admitted into the private space within, moving from the lemonade, one might say, to the sipping whiskey. The front porch, in myth at least, was the place for a rocking chair, a swinging loveseat, a drowsy dog, feeble light, a door with a gauze-curtained window, an iron knocker. Today, paranoia has made of it a security zone, floodlit, with motion detectors, intercoms and peep-holed doors.

The back porch, when present, is as private as the front is social. Where the front surveys the trimmed lawn and the public street, the rear looks onto the yard where children play, the garden that needs weeding, the alley of trashcans, the shed of broken tools: the unflattering backside of people's lives. The ragged grass is diamond-rutted with base paths, the picnic table stained with the green, sticky oil of fallen butternuts. And yet its very lack of presentability links it to the privacy of our thoughts, the confidences and confessions not shared with neighbours in front porch conversation. The moon will rise over these ashcans, and silver the glistening bodies of slugs on the lettuce, emboldening raccoons from the tree to poke into the compost and tip over garbage. We will pour more wine, grateful to have even this poor piece of earth for our own.

KITCHEN

Dominated by twin gods of fire and ice, this room blends art and science, stern law and reckless indulgence. Its talismans: the immeasurably earnest measures, the Sacred Spoons, the Holy Cups, invariable standards willing the wild hunch of today to become the sure thing of tomorrow. And against this rigour, the calls for spontaneity, *a pinch, a hint, a taste, a dash, a splash* – loose passion-talk akin to *a wink, a peck, a nudge, a slap, a tickle*, the vocabulary of flirtation and pursuit.

Warm heart of the house, it rivals the bedroom in sensual pleasure, enticing with licit delights those outside the closed ring of marriage. Its art lies in the whetting of appetites. Drying spices season the breeze through its windows. Ropes of garlic tie us to the earth from which we've sprung. Eating is gusto; the chairs are cracked from rocking-back laughter, the table stained with spilled wine and tears.

Yet this is also the room of knives and cleavers, the butcher's block, coarse altar of dismembering. People are killed here by those who should have split the head of cabbage instead. A place of blood and bread, nurture and recrimination, a place of rising up and punching down. Skinning, cutting, boiling, searing, grinding, pounding – yet also soul-starvation, love doled out in rationed grams and calories. The bitter silences of meals begrudged, meals that grew cold waiting, the gristle-chew of steak burned in anger, the wilful oversalting, the sly, slow murder of butterfat and cream, the watery carelessness of vegetables from cans. If we are what we eat, then, loveless, we are the frozen TV dinner.

LIVING ROOM

The slack, misnamed province of La-Z-Boy, couch potato, boob tube.
Once the glittering parlour, where visitors brought champagne
conversation, the room has dwindled to a microwaved meal and a
beer, a flannel cocoon from which we emerge unchanged. In the gulag
of our own company, we rehash old news, churn ceaseless weather,
envy the perfect bodies of unsporting sports. Yesterday's papers and
magazines, intermittently read, befit the waiting room of a bus depot
or the dentist. A corner with a good chair, good light, good books
offers token resistance, but as the room of canned music and canned
laughter, it remains unconducive to true attention.

Lacking the kitchen's nourishing warmth and fragrance, this
room wastes us away. Stuck fast in the web of habit, unsure if we're
living or dying, we struggle weakly against our fate.

BATHROOM

Rightly called water closet, a small room that, like the body itself, is awash in fluid gurglings – of pipes and taps, of flushed waste, of splashing in the tub, the slathered slap-slop of soap and lather, the shaving, spitting, rinsing and scrubbing, the spraying, dousing, douching, sluicing, soaking. Like the bedroom, a chapel of the body, yet more secret, more shameful – even sexual partners may hide from each other here, praising, bemoaning and primping the self before the glass, painting over flaws, powdering, gargling, spraying away odours, artfully arranging a few wisps of hair into an illusion. Of all inner doors of the house, this one is most likely to lock, so fearful are we of being caught doing what all do, of being found to be what all are. The prospect of visitors sends us into frenzies of scouring: the gleam of porcelain as a measure of virtue.

As the kitchen with its twin deities, so the bathroom with its taps: hot and cold clearly separate and pure. The clever gnome who invented the single bathroom faucet rides a mud-coloured horse, paints all his walls beige, owns a chess set whose pieces and squares are grey.

At its best, it is here that the weary, wounded self is tended with hospice concern, where aching muscles are heated and soaked, where every crevice and pore is permitted a wet, warm caress, where touch-starved skin is reinvigorated by the slick glycerine smoothness of soap, the stone foam of pumice, the rough cat-tongue of loofah.

BEDROOM

Behind this door, a private language, in dialects high and low: ecstatic speaking in tongues, in tooth and claw. Hand questions thigh, breast hushes mouth, lips stifle as often as they whisper. Nails scratch a personal hieroglyphic on the back, teeth brand the throat. Gutter talk insinuates its way down the ear's spiral staircase. The tongue is a snake in the grass, parting the lips, stealing the breath away.

The bed is central, a dais of wild abandon and utter inertia. Here the life-affirming act gives way to poses of battlefield death. The place of shared passion and fantasy, but equally of private, unconfessable dreams, and, too often, of the bitter turning away, cold shoulders back-to-back in a never-wide-enough space. It is the sanctuary of don't-tell, undone by the telling of telephone, television.

How can the incubator of dreams look so ordinary? Tour friends through the house, and it becomes a room like any other, bedsheets and curtain lace as casually notable as the stackable washer-dryer. Does no one blush at the fertility of the pillows that germinate dream-murder and orgies and flying? Is it not unseemly to view the rubbed brass bedstead? Is no one tempted to open the nightstand drawer? Has the boudoir been tamed, our private night-dwelling shrunken to matching lampshades and pillow slips, and *How much did you pay for that?*

Those in touch with the inner world may have a desk here, a small one, for dream journaling, diaries, love notes, the sorts of wordwork done in longhand. What is the writer wearing at this desk when the fleeting communiqués of the dream can still be recalled? None of your business. This is not part of the tour; let us move on.

Besides, it's the moon's room. To be here in daylight is to have to justify overmuch. In those hours, its character shifts like leafshadow on the blind. It becomes the refuge of the tearful, the cave of the hungover and the migraine-victim, the why-bother-leaving comfort of the ambitionless layabout, the pleasure dome of the newlywed, the barren desert of the unloved, the straw-strewn, smelly cage of the wed-too-long, the unescaped, the suicidal.

CLOTHES CLOSET

Adjacent to the spread-eagle playground of nudity, this is the tight-squeeze cell of business suit, uniform and formal wear, the sloppy odorous locker of sweatsuit, spandex and drawstring waistbands. It's the small room of great disappointments, the thin people we no longer are, the fashions we cling to that have long passed. The prison cell of the ego, its only glass throws back an all-season view of the self, a relentless posing parade of disillusion, of the material world gone wrong. It is the shameful hall of bad taste, the embarrassing threadbare wardrobe of a play that's run too long. On the floor are trunks and boxes into which we squeeze a smaller version for the road. The multiplicity of costumes betrays our inability to be happy in any one skin.

CHILD'S ROOM

A ferment. This is the room where change is daily enacted, not merely wished for. In this chaos, the newest person continues her birth, moulting her covering every few months. In cradle, crib, or bed, she is watched through the night by the 20 watt eye of God. Her familiars gather round in solidarity against all rules and expectations; they speak to her in a language we thought was as dead as Aramaic. Birds and fish fly above her, all phyla of creatures crowd near, primary colours proclaim themselves like the banners of Columbus in the New World. Words lengthen on her shelves, her legends complicate, the cave drawings of the species decorate her walls. She alone in the house writes history while remembering none. Of all the house's holy precincts – and each holds its sacred purpose inside, like a seed – this, under all its disorder, is the farthest-looking. Here, the blueprints of the future are drawn up daily. In its cardboard and plastic glory, with its tiny table and chairs, this is the ark and spacecraft of humanity, setting sail for Andromeda. Miracle happens here. Cloud chamber, hothouse, think tank; the manger of God's anointed.

HALLWAY

Where does this passage lead? How long will it take to get there? Like dreamless naps, most are too short and narrow for memorable features. Off-white, diplomatically avoiding clashes with rooms more strongly colour-committed, the hall is a disappointing tunnel of winter against which the kitchen beckons like a tropical holiday. Too short for generations of ancestor portraits, too narrow to offer step-back study of abstract art or landscapes snapped from train windows on longer, more interesting journeys. The hall bears the scars of moving, when the brutal broad shoulders of bulky furniture bulled in and out of more exciting rooms, blackening and chipping its surfaces. It accepts this indifference, and learns to regard itself as something less than the smallest room, though some claim more area, and are entered more often. Highway and game trail of the house, its pride is in its useful-ness. But just once, dreams the hallway, hold the party here, spill the wine on me.

STAIRWAY

The hall's manic-depressive cousin, the ticker-tape of the domestic economy. It rises to the highest level of the house, then sinks back; descends to the lowest depth, but shrinks from hitting rock bottom. The sine wave of the house, indecisive, buffeted by yearning, seeking company one moment, isolation the next, yet on arriving, never entering, but standing on the threshold, as if awaiting an invitation. Ask if it's going up or down, it answers 'Both.' The enemy of the even, the flat, the horizontal, the mundane, at best it pauses briefly and calls it 'landing.'

BASEMENT

This is the subconscious, the foundation of the house. To make it bright and cheery and 'liveable,' to tart it up as 'rec room' or 'family room' or 'exercise room,' is to refuse the unrealized its own domestic space. It is dark, cold and dank for a reason – attention is not meant to shine at all hours, in all corners of the mind. To sterilize this wasteland is to deny the riverflow of homelife a place to silt up. This is the marsh bog of days, the necessary mud-and-sand filter in the psychic ecology of the house. To arrive here is to arrive at the delta of the Big River, the place where the blues was born. It is the unsubtle wrecking yard of all that we should have known would not last: half-hearted hobbies, wobbly furniture, outgrown passions, textbooks that taught us nothing we remember, clever distractions that distract us no more, all the cheap once-a-year tinsel of the spirit. The basement is the bed and pillow of the house, where the years' conflicts and enthusiasms go to lie down and rest a moment, or dismantle themselves forever.

Thus, only a few twilight activities are entitled to corners of the basement. A darkroom, perhaps, where shadows emerge out of watery invisibility. For the darkroom too is a bedroom, the dream-space of the inner eye, a place of total darkness or the lurid red light of sexual exploration. But what shadows take form here should properly have been etched by a needle of light through a pinhole stabbed in a shoebox, not recorded by a state-of-the art single lens reflex in a floodlit studio.

A sauna too would be in keeping with the spirit of the basement, a tight, hot cell in which to sweat out the poisonous atmosphere of the city's working day. Here too light must be dim, little more than candle- or firelight-strength. As in the bedroom and bathroom, our nudity signals arrival at our fundamental selves. This is a fundamental place, a dungeon to which we consign ourselves in hope of repentance and ritual purification, the only vestibule of hell with visiting privileges, a burial chamber from which we pray to emerge resurrected.

Once, loners with limited horizons came to the basement to search out foreign voices, yearning for something they could never name. They hunched over tables illuminated with glowing tubes and dials imagining themselves at the edge of the Milky Way, half-hoping to hear angels or proof of alien intelligence. What they heard through celestial static was soul music, the weather in Finland and news for all the ships at sea. They heard *mariachis* and the voices of drowning sailors. Communing with spirits is a basement activity, but those days have gone.

ATTIC SCRIPTORIUM

Treehouse

Under the peaked cap of the house, two tiny eye-windows stare into elms. An attic treehouse, the city scribbler's substitute for life alone in the woods. Here, like an only child, he surrounds himself with his fetishes and enacts elaborate world-creating rituals. Here he makes his loving withdrawal to a nest of leaf-obscurity, a green hiddenness from which his singing comes. This room above all others suits his peculiar angle of vision. To look out and see only sky, or the organic journaling of trees is to join a bird-and-squirrel world that knows nothing of human ambitions. To look down and see human industry as small, distant and vulnerable is to be smitten with protective feeling, a desire to record and preserve what is earnest and well-intentioned, if often unwise and tightly-horizoned. This word-closet offers privacy of mind as the water-closet offers privacy of body. The banished phone is the antenna of worldly attention pulled in, the rope ladder of the treehouse pulled up.

Hiding Place

Long a place to stash a mad wife, or any socially unacceptable kin, including a scribbler. The place to which the Baal Shem Tov relegated demons. A place to hide from Nazis and door-to-door salesmen, to hide from parents when a child, from a child when a parent. A sky-closet through whose keyhole one vanishes like smoke. Ideally, the room should be secret as in old movies, concealed behind a sliding bookcase. Among cobwebs and a ghostly bridal gown, brave children played hide-and-seek here, hearts pounding. Scribblers do too, though their game is hide *to* seek: hide in solitude seeking connection, in loneliness seeking love.

Den

Place where the grass is down-trodden. Lair of a beast dangerous when disturbed. Cave, where animals dream out the winter or where the first humans daubed the walls with ochre, blood and burnt sticks, to tell tales, to record great hunts, narrow escapes from death, fantastic visions. The cozy, book-lined, leather-chaired sanctuary of the sherry-sipping class, but equally, the disreputable hole of the poor, the addicted, the criminal: den of thieves, opium den, den of iniquity.
     The scribbler's room is all of these, and more.

Monastic

Under one roof with the rest of domesticity, the attic is *in* the world but not *of* it, its occupant unreachable, squirreled away in the only cranny that family life has not toyed with, TV'd, CD'd, videoed, Holly Hobbied, geegawed or tarted up for guests. Set apart, not visited without purpose or effort. A ground-level study looking onto the garden is pleasant enough; an office off the kitchen is convenient for tea and toast to coddle the genteel. But the attic, more distant from family life, acknowledges human weakness in proximity to distraction. It knows the writer's blocked if he peers down the block for the postman, calculating when the flap-knock of mail slot will come. So the attic thwarts temptation with the discipline of stern elevation, demands he become an ascetic atop a pole. It's a confessional without the assurance of forgiveness, or even of an answering voice. Stifling in summer, freezing in winter, lonely year round, the scriptorium is a cell, a punishment for speaking out of turn, which in turn permits it. Meteora without the monastic community or the tour buses, a mountain cave for one, the attic shelters the urban hermit, the family anchorite. Being locked in would be all right too.

Paper

Long before the scribbler lugged up his reams of White Laid Bond, this was already paper space, the natural blotter of the house, filter on the furnace of family life. Cellulose lies between raw joists, trapping the adult hot air of argument and the temper tantrum of the child. The room has absorbed generations of screams and curses, passionate pleading, the lilt of lullaby and the hoarse whispers of make-up sex. Here, on the edge of the world-text, the scribbler becomes his marginalia. Love letters and immigration papers age in their steamer trunk, fermenting to a nostalgia potent enough to induce tears and drunken singing. National blood-feuds flame into wars in the reports of foreign correspondents, now crumbling in a stack of brittle dailies. One corner shelters a great paper brain that once buzzed with insect thought. But though the room is an archive of paperwork, the one scrap it lacks is a building permit. The make-word space is make-do. Bookcases crawl round knee walls unable to stand erect, let alone dream of the dizzy heights of those floor-to-ceiling, laddered, book-orchard libraries. The desk is what will fit, or can be built to fit, never to be removed. The room's lack of conformity to local codes merges with that of its occupant, adding illegality and secrecy to the eccentricity and folly which all profitless writing shares.

Shape

Before the scribbler chooses a first word, a first letter, the space itself chooses. It begins at the beginning; it speaks its shape: A. Bent to his task by the sloping walls, the scribbler conforms to his space. Impressionable, he takes the imprint of A; he also begins. No matter how pre-saturated with love or hate, violence or tenderness, no matter how waspishly elaborate his paper constructions become, this space will always remind him he is just a beginner.

Lookout

Tell the truth but tell it slant. Sloping walls support certain inclinations, give the voice a particular pitch. Emerging from his tented room, into the company of foursquare, settled folk, the scribbler speaks in the accent of an outlander, displays the social awkwardness of the hermit, the restlessness of the nomad. He returns to bright civilized life blinded, dazed and sub-verbal, like one who's lived too long among animals, been lost for years in the desert or adrift on the sea. On his long watch in the crow's nest of the family ship, he has stared at the featureless page waiting for something to break the surface: a white whale, a treasure island, a lost Atlantis.

Mystic Consciousness

To *climb* the stairs is truer for this room than to *walk* up them, the rise-to-run ratio so extreme that one is obliged to use feet *and* hands, as on a ladder. This is as it should be. The ladder was good enough for angels, or so Jacob dreamed. The attic is a special level of consciousness in the collective mind of the house, and passage into it *should* involve this all-fours humbling of oneself to the task. Ritual purification. We wash our hands and remove our shoes, we bend to enter the low door of the Japanese teahouse; we prostrate ourselves on the floors of certain temples. Sacred trance, hallucination, prayer and meditation happen here. Holy precincts.

Roots

Hairline cracks in the plaster of old attic rooms are the roots of heaven, by which the realm of the spirit grips the solid earth of the house. The attic is thus the root-cellar of heaven, its roof the sky-twin to the sloped root-cellar door. Attic and basement have always been kin – the tainted-air tombs of the house, the acknowledged frontiers, the outer reaches. Border states in the empire of the everyday, they are rough, neglected places that, even if made habitable, never become conventional, retain always the character of the stranger.

TOOL SHED

TOOL SHED

The first warm weekend blossoms with ambition: build a trellis, a fence, a picnic table; rake grass; clean gutters; prune; turn the earth; plant. After months of frozen shut, the shed springs open.

We're never tool-shed. They're always around, and like children, they model their character on us. If we're careless, we have to search them out; they're found sleeping in the long grass, or leaning in neglected corners, shiftless layabouts who stub out cigarettes reluctantly when the boss comes in. If we're religious, we find them hanging like a saviour just where we left them, whenever we need them.

Real tools are old, archetypal. On winter streets, a few clever Jacks flaunt their smart shovels, the ones bent like a straw at the waterline. They get their digs in, bragging with every mouthful, 'You *can* reinvent the wheel.' As bodies grow weaker in each generation, the tool-making mind grows more cunning. No back-breaking labour for these college boys.... But theirs are petty changes. True, the rough types in the shed have refined house-bound cousins who work small and light, yet the family of diggers includes both spade and spoon, and the family of spearers both pitchfork and pie fork, each tribe tracing its origins back to a single austere patriarch, who, like the grandfather of the aborigine, was born in the beginning. Adam, after all, was a gardener. Unlike those bastard gadgets in the infomercials, the outlines of essential tools are iconic, as constant, familiar and suggestive as letters of an alphabet, despite the variety of fonts. They have written themselves decisive moral roles to play in our oldest stories.

One is of a wolf disguised as a grandmother, who eats an incautious girlchild, who in turn is rescued by a woodchopper who axes the wolf open so the girl may jump out, whole. Another tells of a man who will keep all the land he can travel round in a day, who runs ever farther in his greed and falls down dead in the evening, his mouth full of blood, his land reduced to the six feet of dirt shovelled over him in the end. Tools frown on human carelessness, on avarice, on dreamy notions, indecision, idleness and self-indulgence. Stern Hutterites of the household, they stand aloof from toys and comfort; they believe life is work, and best done together. Their interdependent collective of tool shed, -box, or -belt is their sign that there is no single all-purpose gadget. There is nothing to debate or mull over; the commandments came down long ago, and do not change. Innovation – novelty – is regarded with suspicion. We are peasants, they tell us, all made in God's image: squat and big-boned, shaped for endurance, not vanity. Destined for heavy duty, our useful lives will end when we're splintered and broken.

Yet after decades of abrasion and the sweat of gripping hands, see how beautifully they turn silver and smooth under human touch. For a fleeting instant they shine like saints, triumphant in the purity of their mute suffering. It is then, if there is a god, they should be taken up.

FORK

Stabs the clod as its pansy cousin stabs meat from a plate. Equally at home in Neptune's ocean and the Devil's hell, therefore an elemental tool: earth, water, fire. Prick of conscience, goad to all flesh, which is grass. Companion to the scythe, grim reaper's instrument.

RAKE

Bony fingers of a skinny arm, harrowing the dirt as though buried
alive. Skeletal bird – heron, flamingo – chicken-scratching for corn
that never fattens. Rips passionless scars in the earth's back; hardly
the sensualist its namesake claims to be. Combs its fingers through
the uncut hair of the lawn, to claw up the scurf. But back in the shed,
has little to report: a lost toy or key, broken bones from a tree's
struggle with the wind.

SPADE

Trump card of the garden, ace of black soil. What cuts deepest, stabs
to the root, unafraid of what might be unearthed. Won't shy away
from dirty work, not too proud to dig in, to muck about. Comes out
with cold clay clinging. Partner in crime to gumboots and rolled-up
sleeves. Knows where all the bodies are buried. Grave tool: the very
epitome of plain speaking: we must call it what it is.

HAMMER

Stubby steel finger driving home the point, fixing it in place, jabbing an opponent's chest, *See HERE, you ain't goin' NOWHERE*. Settling the argument once and for all, hitting the nail on the head and circling it for emphasis. Hates to admit mistakes; claws them back with a scream, with a grudge. When it comes to destruction, bigger is better. A real thug, a fist pounding out frustrations, smashing down all opposition. Natural demagogue: a single hammer dominates a million nails.

NAIL

Indistinguishable from his fellows in the bag. Bought by the pound; cannon fodder; the perfect individual victim. A straight arrow, a pinhead. Point him where you want him to go, he shows no initiative, but waits for you to drive him there, as dim-witted sheep wait passively for the shepherd. Ubiquitous, despised, useful in his place, he accepts in his heart the doctrine that whoever stands out will be beaten down. With each stroke, his head lowers till he's totally abased. A dutiful citizen in the grip of the state, he puts up only token resistance, and disappears into his work, flush with successful submission.

SAW

Rip. Hand. A wolf gets its way with sharp teeth. The wider the smile, the more dangerous. Hack. Buck. Chews its victims to fine dust.

HORSES

Feet in the grass but never eating, what else could they be but skeletal? They lack the spirit to gallop and will not pull, yet sleep standing up and have strength to bear all manner of burdens between them. The screams of the saw and banging of hammers cannot startle them, blinkered to all but each other. In tandem, the very models of forbearance, a working team, yoked in rigid marriage, able to endure all labour, all confinement so long as it be shared. In a crowded shed, one is sometimes found mounting the other, but woodenly – neither shows pleasure, and like mules, they are sadly infertile. Should one break its back or a leg, its life of service ends. The mate inevitably pines away, useless in singularity: one wooden horse with nothing inside, a creature bereft, fit only for the child cowboy.

PLUMB BOB

So obvious, so simple, it scarcely needed inventing. Perhaps a kid designed it: a top on a string, a tool like a toy. Who else would have given a thing so enslaved to gravity such a light-hearted moniker? Something so earnest, obsessed with the dead straight, should be Robert to you. But no, this one wears his expertise casually. Plumb Bob, like Joey Bananas, is a strict enforcer with a fruity name.

LEVEL

Partner to Plumb Bob, and like him, both sober and whimsical.
Among construction tools, how many claim as their only moving part
a bubble, captured champagne souvenir? What's next? Moonbeam
callipers? A firefly-powered trouble-light? The unicorn-horn auger? Yet
there's authority in this thermometer with its liquid inside, which we
peer at for proof of what we've already guessed. Its pill-shaped
window contains a solution, but the prescription is level-headed and
ever the same: think flat, look to the horizon, suppress all natural
inclinations.

SQUARE

Among sticklers for precision, this is the ultimate stick-in-the-mud; its name declares its inflexible nature. Not loopy or bubble-brained, this one is positively rigid, unyielding, take-it-or-leave-it. A stern father, he runs his unit on military lines, and demands obedience; his arms are not meant for hugging. Others may know all the angles – this drill sergeant claims only his is right, and will maintain this position forever. Stability is all, he says. Straighten up. Square those shoulders. Tool of our fallen, civilized state, he forgets that God draws no straight lines. That before we lived square, we lived round, in the paper sphere of the wasp, the bowl-shaped nest of the bird, the spiral shell of the mollusc. That, for a brief moment, even humans were permitted in the charmed circle of mud hut, igloo, tepee and yurt.

AWL

Or nothing. A yawn, a drawl, an *aw shucks*. A real sharpie, or just a
bore? Handyman or one-trick wonder? Y'all come back when y'all
decide.

WEDGE & SLEDGE

Two brothers in the persuasion business. The smart one sticks his nose
in, ruthless as a compass needle, finding fault, pointing out cracks in
each united front, chinks in the armour. The other, the heavyweight,
the forceful personality, falls upon weakness, drives hard and fast
down the shortest road to Splitsville.

HEDGE CLIPPERS

The shears of Atropos, a garden-variety Fate, enforce an iron
standard, write a withering line. Any upstart green life that knows not
its place will find its flowering snapped in two with this judgement. Its
blades remind us tools are cousins to weapons, intent on violence.
Two knives working in concert, twin guillotines lopping off heads.

LAWN ROLLER

The law 'n order fascist of the tool shed, master of brute force. Might is right. Soft words and caresses carry no weight. Some substantial impression must be made on these unruly sods. To keep them in line, and in their place. To keep them down.

LADDER

Jacob's went up to heaven, and each one since has been hoping. The portable staircase leans and points out the way, rungs aching in antici-pation. God-yearning aside, this one would settle for a lady's balcony, the fragrant welcoming limbs of apple trees, a hayloft with dust motes dancing in air. But it's always the gutters, rain gutters dammed with wet-black leaves and rotting butternuts. The heights should mean more, much more than this. Still, it could be worse. Contrary to that game with the snakes, ladders don't always rise. Imagine the grief and shame of the ladder lowered into an open grave.

TROWEL

Intimate implement, tool of modest aspiration. Not standoffish, it closes the distance its long-handled brothers insist on, humbles its user to an attitude of prayer in respect to the earth. A supplicant shovel, it draws the proud hand down to the fragrant rot of compost, consecrating the living and the dead within a bent-arm arc as close as a kiss or an embrace. Kneel in the garden. Feel the body heat of earth on your knees; welcome its darkness inside you, in the cracks of your skin, under your nails. Later, as you bend to wash up, catch yourself in the bathroom mirror, forehead branded with its black sign, where you paused in planting to wipe away the sweat. You are marked, as on Ash Wednesday. Dedicated. You are shown for what you have always been, the earth's own, and the lowly leveller, the trowel, has spoken this truth to your face.

NEIGHBOURHOOD SHOPS

THE STREET

The street was once a fast-running stream; now it's a backwater, each shop its own flyblown, stagnant pool. No high-tech security cameras watch over them. Duct tape is enough to hold the shaky panes of cracked glass in grimy display windows when there's no point to breaking in. *Going Out of Business* sales can last a decade or more in this neighbourhood, as each proprietor's resolve softens, and the stores slip weakly from going concerns to hobby rooms. Their meagre trade justifies no employees beyond their owner-operators, most often men, whittling away at their life-long occupations rather than face the enforced boredom of official retirement. If *the business of America is business*, the business of these men is killing time. Stockboys of twilight, they are content to let the inventory deplete itself by infinitesimal increments without replacement. Their kids are already through college, their mortgages paid off, and their government pensions, though small, are at least regular. The upstairs apartment covers the few remaining expenses. Even when someone else owns the building, the rents on these blocks are so low, and the merchandise so cheap, that *overhead* refers mainly to falling plaster.

Hours

With so little financial incentive, these shops open entirely on whim. If you find the door unlocked, enter slowly, so as not to startle the one-time go-getter dozing in a chair after lunch. The handwritten *Back in 10 minutes* sign might mean forty minutes or an hour, but it's not intended for you anyway; it's a signal to the wife, if she's dropped by with coffee, that he's close by somewhere, keep looking, maybe down

51

at Donut Time or the post office. But neither is it unusual, with these motivationless owners, for this morning's *Open* sign to hang on the door right next to last night's *Sorry We're Closed*, in perfect accidental expression of the now deep-seated ambivalence about trade in general.

Signage

This waning entrepreneurial enthusiasm is reflected in storefronts that haven't been painted in decades. Decoratively festooned with cobwebs and layered in dust, the red-and-yellow cardboard *Sale* signs have lost their once-hysterical enthusiasm, and have greyed into the generic streetscape. They might as well read *Store* for all the attention they attract now.

Confusing all but the regular customer, shops often bear three or four different names, their proprietors lacking the energy to take down the signage of previous owners. So an establishment may display a schizophrenic identity, being at once the Moonlight Laundry, Stella's Confectionary, Corner Video and Al's Convenience. Criminals have fewer aliases.

Hand-lettered signs full of misspellings, illogic and ambiguous communication are commonplace. The all-day breakfast is available till 10 a.m. The jeweller wants your old gold and watch's. The appliance store specializes in all makes and models. The tailor, fittingly, has a three bedroom suit for rent. The hardware store, bristling with rakes and hos, announces the upcoming Boy Scout Manure sale. The grocery's announcement that THIS SAFE IS

ALARMED seems to invite the rejoinder 'I'm a little anxious myself,' while the notice WE WILL BE CLOSE FROM 11 AM TO 3 PM, may further heighten the paranoia of the sensitive reader.

A few proprietors with vestigial pride, who resent the chains, the box stores and e-sales for killing the family business, post handwritten notices saying *We specialize in you, the customer* – which means they have so little to do all day that they'll happily spend a half hour rummaging round in the back for you trying to locate an item that won't profit them more than a quarter, though they're pretty sure they haven't made 'em like that for years. It's this warm, personal, if ultimately fruitless attention that makes the backwater business so dear to the hearts of local seniors and others intimidated by the loud music, ignorant young salespeople and seductive displays of the more competitive marketplaces of the malls and the downtown.

CLOTHING STORE

Few nowadays have seen the inside of this store – or wish to. Ancient mannequins, the soles of their feet cruelly pierced with grey metal spikes, appal passers-by with the rictus of their smiles. Innocent bystanders of countless wars, more than a few lack arms. Many have fingers, toes, or noses missing, as though stricken with a commercial form of leprosy. Their wigs, like those of their owner, have a dull, bird's-nest quality. Their clothes, an indestructible polyester, are at least a decade or two out of date. They grimace unceasingly at the flapping wings of rain, sun, snow, wind and the dark. They seem to know something the proprietor has yet to acknowledge. A few have tipped their pedestals, and now lean, naked and bald, in soiled corners, where they stare at the floor like catatonics, or up toward the ceiling, arms perpetually outstretched, as if beseeching their maker to gather them back to his bosom at the end of their long-suffering and uncomplaining service.

USED APPLIANCE STORE

If you share with the owner a tactile appreciation of cold materials –
metal, plastic, glass – this is a shop not without its own sensual
beauty. In the front window, disconnected stove top elements tangle
in heaps like the breeding balls of snakes. Examined individually, their
whorls might be the cold metal fingerprints of forty years of dead
stoves, and the owner the forensic pathologist that can identify yours.
A few working models with 90-day guarantees are displayed on the
sidewalk for inspection; by its colour alone, an avocado fridge
declares the precise period of its vogue.

BARBER SHOP

The nearest alternative is on the frontier of the neighbourhood, a 'salon' where a 15- minute cut is primped and gussied into something close to an hour. The ritual seems to involve a choice of herbal teas and at least two different echelons of attendants with piercings and multi-coloured hair. Customers draped in fuchsia bedsheets pour out confessions about their love lives while skinny stylists of indetermi-nate gender flit about their heads like gnats, their impossibly tiny scissors making snipping noises and producing scarcely any hair to be swept away. The walls are covered in an assortment of edgy artworks, and triangular tables are strewn with Helmut Newton photo albums or magazines where the ads for shampoos and make-up outnumber the articles.

By contrast, this place is handy and cheap. Its decor reminds you of the barber shop of your youth, where on Saturday afternoons, men who hadn't had hair in 20 years sat on chrome-and-plastic waiting chairs, perpetually deferring their next-in-line status, arguing about Hull and Howe in the six-team National Hockey League. Moribund, this place lacks that buzz. You've noticed this guy dozing in his big swivel chair, watching ballgames on a portable TV or passing the afternoon grooming himself with the aid of artful mirror arrange-ments. Judging from his own hair, he's a firm believer in the comb-over and some light-reflecting form of pomade. You chalk up the enthusiasm of his greeting to boredom.

But some commerce not declared on the sign underlies this enterprise, like a deadhead bobbing below the surface, waiting to punch a hole in your boat. A code is spoken here which you've missed entirely. There's a table full of *Sports Illustrated*, some stale *Time* and 'men's magazines.' The mistress of days is a busty woman in a bikini, a harem girl schooled to repeat forever the name of the auto repair potentate who magnanimously bequeathed her to this establishment. She is replaced monthly with others of different hair and eye colour, but identical proportions. They all propose something lascivious, having convinced themselves, against all the evidence, that you're not a fat, balding, middle-aged chump of limited economic resources. The earnest '50s manliness of the place is an atmosphere as identifiable as the stink of a locker room, and its childhood familiarity creates the illusion of safety. It's only later you consider that, like the linen draped round you in the chair, it cloaks and hides more than it declares.

For there comes a moment during the process when the barber leans in too close. It occurs to you – now that you're forced to think – that a haircut involves an unseemly, far-too-intimate form of attention. Thank God you didn't accept the offer of shampoo or a shave. He seems to rub himself below the belt on the thick arm-pommel of the leather chair in which you, the customer-victim, have been costumed, noosed and briefly enthroned. Should your hand be resting there, a split-second of perverse, electric, linen-shrouded contact jerks you like a hooked fish, unsure if this was accidental, but unwilling to find out. You leave convinced that the posters that lovingly idealize the haircuts of twelve-year-old boys and the fastidi-ous beard trims of doe-eyed, rosy-lipped twenty-year-olds have more than a strictly commercial purpose; that despite the jock talk and the women displaying their cleavage, the shop's true gods are those fey young men whose meticulously groomed heads decorate the walls like hunting trophies.

HARDWARE STORE

The owner sits back and watches the cars cold-shoulder their way to Home Depot and Colour Your World. If someone stops, it will be to buy – what? No business survives on the profits from rubber washers, nickel screws and magnetized spare-key containers. The shovels do well when a blizzard dumps three feet of snow unexpectedly, and the dixie-cup-spoons folks keep in the trunk won't dig out their cars for the drive to Canadian Tire. In late summer, Mason jars are still popular with the few aging Old World gardeners whose wives continue to put up tomatoes or dill pickles, and have underestimated the crop. But this place is really the male equivalent of the beauty parlour or the coffee klatch – a place for men to lean on the counter and swap stories, give advice or speculate about how to accomplish this task or that: how long is your ladder, how big is your hammer, what wiring have you got. The hangers-on are the same species that live on every street, who cannot let a renovation, tree trimming or sewer repair occur without coming over to inspect the work, pass judgement and ask how much that tool set you back. *You can't do it like that. Damn thing'll break. When I did mine ...*

SHOE REPAIR

The verdicts of this judge are three in number: a new heel for five dollars; a new sole for ten; don't bother, it's not worth it. You might visit this establishment once a year and get the same claim ticket every time; he keeps it by the cash near the newspaper. But in truth, you don't need it – he'll remember your face. Your shoe doesn't interest him; they don't make good shoes anymore, and his father made them from scratch. He doesn't stock laces, though there are a few singles in a box thrown under the counter. It helps to like brown; for anything else, try the drugstore. The shelves are full of unclaimed footwear from forty years of business, and when he can't find yours, it's because he figured you weren't coming back either. If you want a yellowish size-thirteen cowboy boot or a woman's purple mule, make him an offer. Beware the disturbing models of feet with their dusty bones revealed.

SHOE STORE

Don't try to rob the place; there's next to nothing in the till, and besides, her description of you would be precise – you're the only customer she's seen in weeks. You wait, idly inspecting a few modern, tumorous running shoes, while she tells Fran two or three times that she'll "have to call back later, I have a customer. No, really!" Having all the while sized up your feet with a professional eye, she puts down the phone and lets out a delighted "EEEE" as she runs to the back. You imagine she's seen a mouse – a not unlikely possibility, given the age of the building. When she returns with boxes of shoes and, inexplicably, desert boots in "your size," you break her heart. Sorry, we don't carry laces, she says; perhaps the drugstore.

DRUGSTORE

Long eclipsed by Shoppers Drug and PharmaSave, it specializes in those perverse rubber devices only old folks understand or require. The pharmacy has a devoted clientele, among the aged, because it's prepared to pay the seniors' $2.00 dispensing fee, and among those on psychiatric medication, who bond with the staff during long, meandering conversations that fill the empty hours of both parties. They carry no shoelaces. They have given up trying to compete in diapers, cosmetics, toothpaste, shampoo, school supplies, candy, pop … items that require great space for their endless variety, and demand younger staff, knowledgeable about fashion. Their concession to modernity is to offer 7¢ copier service for those who find the library's 25¢ a bit steep. They claim to deliver. Likely by bicycle.

BANKS

Money shrinks from failure, as the healthy inch away from sweat-stained coughers on the bus. There were once four banks in as many blocks; now there is one, whose 19th century limestone stairs declare that arthritic seniors and people pushing baby buggies have no money worth troubling with, and deserve to be loaned none. The chiselled inscription in the stone façade translates as *Fuck off – cash your cheque at Money Mart, or stash it under the mattress.*

The first bank to close morphed into a dollar store, the steel-lined vault safeguarding a new treasury of cheap plastic. The second condescended to cash pension cheques on Tuesdays; now, apparently, Capital has declared Tuesdays uneconomic. The third empty bank, like a songbird promising spring, chirps *New store opening soon!* Except this bird is stuffed, layered in dust, and spring, like Tuesdays, has been cancelled.

What's left is a machine and an eye in the ceiling that watches money come and go and never forgets a face with a stolen card. What's left is the litter of envelopes in which you feed your cheque to the machine, and the receipts the machine spits at you after eating your money. What's left are your neighbours idly noting how much it takes to carry you for the week. What's left are the papers they read and discard while you try making your back and shoulders broader than a PIN.

DOLLAR STORE

There are actually two of these in the neighbourhood, facing each other across the main drag like gunfighters duelling to see who will run Tombstone. But unlike in the old west, this town *is* big enough for the both of them, and more besides. Apparently no depressed neighbourhood can have enough cheap plastic, even if it's the same cheap plastic in each store. The wholesaler who peddles identical glue traps, fake Tupperware and costume jewellery to these retailers walks in the footsteps of tinkers and snake oil salesmen.

Nonetheless, these stores are handy for parents of kids under ten. For next to nothing, you can scrape together enough tinsel and bric-a-brac to fill the loot bags for your daughter's birthday party, though the life span of products sold here is measured in minutes. Buy your child a heart-shaped lacquerware box for Valentine's, and when you peel off the bar code sticker, the lacquer tears off in a ragged strip. With price the sole organizing factor, this is the only store that could logically associate a rubber snake, snack food, tampons, and penlight batteries. Outside, under the awning, are CUSSIONS 3 for $1, and apocalyptic warnings about the consequences of trying on the T-shirts.

SAWDUST SHOP

Defined, in the hand-lettered royal 'we,' solely by what it does not: *We do not sell furniture. We do not cut wood for people. We do not make change for the bus. We* is a knotted, gnarled man, who on sunny days takes the air in front of the shop with his improbable fluffy dog, a scrap creature apparently made from frayed rope and floor sweepings. There is an empty chair – *Don't sit down* – next to the empty bookshelves – *This is not a public library*. The wood-shaving dog yaps away potential customers interested in – what? Piles of sawdust? Bookshelves and cabinets not for sale? Empty tobacco tins on the shelves? We's lungs are slowly filling with cellulose; he's becoming a tree again, his hat a bird's nest. The rough bark of perpetual annoyance is his stock-in-trade.

With time on his hands, he carries on a wooden and silent dialogue with his neighbours through his forest of crabby signs. *Have a nice day BUT NOT HERE. No public phone. No public washrooms.* As if documenting some progressive dementia, he continually adds new prohibitions in pencil to warnings already seared into the wood: *No boosters, drug pushers or rubber-neckers wanted. We do not buy hot goods.* He's tired of all these peckerheads. Don't ax him the time of day. This ain't infirmation. He's a materialist, with little curiosity about man or God. He's already built his own pine box. If he wakes in heaven in front of Jesus Christ, his only question will be "What does the H. stand for?" Oddly enough, one sign, fallen flat and buried in a pile of shavings, displays what was presumably the shop's original name: *PINE WITH RAY*. But this failed Ray of sunshine has apparently long forgotten that he once, inadvertently, invited others to share his private longing for better days.

MARTIAL ARTS ACADEMY

Off-hours, a fist on the door says SORRY, its clenched fingers demonstrating the self-evident WE'RE CLOSED. In the window, there are homilies about perseverance, strength, character – qualities required, presumably, to sustain a relative latecomer's business optimism in a neighbourhood where people resist paying to learn anything, and prefer to settle arguments with a frying pan or a beer bottle.

BAKERY

Bread is the staff of life for this business, having conceded the lucrative donut trade to the chain down the street. In the window, a white, tiered wedding cake has acquired a frosting of dust on all its yellowing cardboard-and-Styrofoam surfaces. The pink rosettes have greyed, and the miniature bride and groom are embedded to the ankles in icing like Mob victims in wet cement. No one remembers the last order for one of these monstrosities. Perhaps people no longer believe in marriage, frightened off by the grim omen of these stiffs gazing not at each other but at the larger world passing them by.

ANTIQUE STORE

Though it calls itself 'antique,' this is hardly the neighbourhood one can expect to turn up a Louis XIV chair or a Massachusetts Bay Psalm Book. This is a glorified junk shop whose owner has cottoned on to nostalgia, that almost magical power whose commercial value cannot be overestimated. His best-selling items have always been those produced during the childhood of the purchaser. Their quality need be no better than that of a Coke bottle, a tin bread box or formica table, yet he's free to charge far more than they've ever been worth – free to charge, as they say, whatever the market will bear. Because no one can bear living, bereft of talismans, in the one-dimensional now, without tangible connection to their past.

These objects sell themselves with their textures and smells; to run a hand over them is to rub the genie's lamp, and unleash a palpable sense of loss. You wander in idly, no intention whatever of buying. Yet one glimpse of a certain item can make you feel cheated of your birthright. *Mother gave me one like that when I was seven.* Whether you threw it out, broke it, sold it or lost it – none of that matters now. What matters is that it was yours, was meant to be yours, and would be still, if the world were fair. You ache for it back, to restore the lost balance of your life, the security of a time when you were loved, when life was straightforward, when the simple, homely and unbeautiful were nonetheless charged with a certain strength and could hold all the elements of the world in their rightful relation. If you ask what governs the pricing of these items, the owner will answer simply, "Supply and demand." But you cannot *demand* your past back, you can only yearn for it, fondle it, offer what you can afford, and hope it's enough.

BIRD SHOP

Probably a spare room, a growth on the side of the business next door. The place doesn't actually sell birds, or indeed anything one can see, but the barren stage contains one item of interest: a strange feathered creature on a dead tree perch. The size of a crow, it's so utterly motionless that passing children debate whether it might be stuffed. Excited cries when the bird is reported to have blinked. There is no food in evidence, or droppings beneath the perch. Perhaps it's the mummified spirit of the street, a kind of vulture that will waken when these shops are finally bulldozed, when the last pensioned-off businessman gives in to gentrification and shuffles off to make way for latté shops, high-end sporting goods stores and restaurants with tablecloths.

THE MALL

MALLED

There is a map, and a legend, as befits a quest.

The upper level, should you go there, is a heaven of ideal beauty: graceful furniture, perfect clothes; silver and gold, jewels of every colour and shape. It is quiet. People hover over you, flapping their little wings and watching you don't steal anything, because this material heaven is intended only for the rich.

There is a hell. It's noisy, and stinks of toilets and quick-and-dirty food. No one will notice you there.

At the moment, you are Ground. Whether -down with worry, or -up as fodder, has yet to be determined, but either way you are backdrop, not Figure. You imagine yourself the actor, not the acted upon. You believe in lightning raids on this hostile territory, that, like a magpie, you can make off with some shiny trinket to brighten your nest. But this is *their* labyrinth; enter it and be changed. All their cunning lured you here, and designed these complex pathways to ensnare you. They have known all along you would come. See, a treasureless X marks their self-evident victory: *You are here.*

IN SLEEP COUNTRY

We come to this country exhausted, but cannot sleep. We perch fully dressed, bounce a little, then lie back and confess to the ceiling – impassive as a shrink or a priest – what we desperately want. We've not had a good night in months, tossing and turning, all elbows and knees, knotting ourselves in our sheets, grinding our teeth. We wake aching, as though dragged in our dreams over uneven ground. Hollow-eyed, we stumble, more than willing to fall into sweet oblivion. Nearby, other customers whisper their nightly needs. A blonde-haired girl finds one too hard, another too soft. On the Princess model, it seems she's detected a pea. But the place might be a daycare or a flophouse, dozens of naked mattresses with lights burning all the time and no shut-eye.

 O the pathos of the shop-worn demonstrator – greasy-headed and soiled from sleeping with all comers! But how can one test such an object without driving it round the night sky, grinding its gears, revving up to top speed and slamming on the brakes? Of its forty-wink capacity, have we measured so much as an eye-twitch with our decorous public posing in the fetal position, our Hallmark-card version of angelic child-sleep? What do we know of a bed without praying at its edge, without rutting in it? Is there a brand fit for doggie-style *and* the soul-weight of *Now I lay me*. Will this one support our ascent to heaven, will this one break our fall? There is no rest for the wicked; the only pure sleep is in a manger. We yearn for a bed of roses, but are fated for a bed of stones, a bed of nails. We should learn to sleep like samurai, on the floor with a worn wooden pillow, or in a thistle field, with helmets under our heads.

 Buy one, and they'll donate your old mattress to charity. Pity the homeless who lie on that nightmare-stained pallet! It's a garden plot whose soil is seeded night after night, a blotter soaked in psychic substance, rancid with sweat and the nocturnal emissions of the mind as well as the body. A river-treadmill of the unconscious, where we try to crawl upstream, but remain suspended just beneath the surface. As the ghost to the house, so the dreamlife to the bed. Woe to the beggar who finds his cup filled with this wealth of phantoms, who sleeps even one night in another man's dreams, who rises in the morning haunted by second-hand demons, with someone else's night terrors woven into his hair.

SILVER CITY

In Silver City, the heads of gods and goddesses are eight feet tall and glow from within. Their beautiful purpose is to instill envy. Their stories are distractions; the sound of their weapons is deafening. When you emerge, blinking, into the light, you have undergone mass re-education. Independent thought has been screened out of you. Brand names have been branded on your subconscious. By the grace of crafty product placement, you have been born again in the image of the mall.

HOUSE OF KNIVES

Kirk's a sharp little prick who's given his lifeblood to this business. And working around cold steel, his conversation has become pointed and painful. He's been sliced more times than he cares to remember. He wears no gloves, no chain-mail or Kevlar; he's dying the death of a thousand cuts. Day after day, he stabs himself putting on his nametag and unsheathes the latest refinement of primitive anger. He splits hairs, silk scarves and matchsticks to prove a point. He has them short and long, ones that will cut through shoe leather and bone. He's carrying a switchblade somewhere on his person right now. He has knives for your belt, knives for your butter, steak knives, bread knives, carving knives, hunting knives, gutting knives, pocket knives and a Bowie knife known as an Arkansas toothpick. He has Japanese cooking knives and samurai swords, curved Islamic scimitars, Gurkhas from India, stilettos from the red light districts of Rome and Marseilles, machetes from South America for cutting sugar cane and paths through the jungle. He has tiny conniving knives made by the tricky Swiss that unfold into little porcupines of usefulness; with one knife you can poke holes in leather, fillet a fish, burn paper, open cans and feed pablum to the baby. Like a street thug, Kirk has gotten all that he owns with a knife. He lives by the blade and will surely die that way.

HOUSE OF CARDS

At the cash, the part-time Goth girl is counting the days. Every day is somebody's 'special day.' Or some body's: *in deepest sympathy*. You must play the cards you get, however bogus. There are countless one-of-a-kinds like you, perfect wives, world's greatest dads. Insincerity is the hallmark of this place, its trite rhymes, its forced humour, its cheap lace-and-ribbons sentiment, its obligatory *thank you*s. Someone's always marrying, or pregnant, or turning sweet sixteen – sometimes all at once, though no one card covers that. Bored to death, she curses mothers, fathers, the improbable favourite nephew; she curses St. Patrick, St. Valentine, St. Nick, All Saints, and doodles up a card in honour of Judas. She forgets Remembrance Day, idles on Labour Day and never gives thanks at Thanksgiving. Her palms itch on Palm Sunday; she passes over Passover. Celebrating the Day of the Dead would suit her fine, but she knows the social niceties will crumble soon enough. Her surly generation will inherit the earth, and this place will come tumbling down like ... well, you know.

TOYS Я US

Toys are not us. Toys are her. We're the job, the mortgage, the gastric ulcer, spiralling credit card debt. We're identity theft, kiddie porn, the cut-up parents of missing children. We're all the body parts or weapons you can cram in a gym bag. We're immunizations, all-hazard insurance, homeland security, micro-chip ID. We're the twin towers of western capital, more vulnerable than U.S. Steel ever dreamed. We're exploding sneakers and unclaimed luggage. We're high blood pressure, asthma, tainted water, mad cows in plague piles. We're AIDS and SARS and weapons of mass destruction, playground equipment made water-resistant with cancer-causing agents. Toys are not us. Fears are us. Mother, Father, Child: the nuclear warhead family. Will anyone ever be frivolous again? We offer her jump ropes, bicycles, soccer balls, board games, and she chooses instead manageable domestic worlds of her own devising. Her house is a shoebox firetrap. She stares into it with a focus as intense as an electron microscope. There's a tiny family, tiny beds, even a tiny spotless toilet. Her mother's a part-time veterinarian, fire-fighter and figure skater. Dad plays a musical instrument that only their miniature poodle can hear. Her daughter wears beautiful painted-on clothes, talks on a plastic-chip cell phone. Her toys even have toys. What the mall can't provide, she crafts herself; supper simmers in a bottle-cap frying pan. Her people have names, birthdays, hair styles, favourite colours. Their problems, we overhear, are ours, only lighter and smaller, with friend-lier neighbours. Perhaps toys are us after all. At night, she borrows the flashlight and sets the sun down over their heads, then switches on the fluorescent moon to see them through the night. Her work is playing out our lives. When those lives become hers, she'll be ready.

Acknowledgements

Thanks to the Canada Council, the Ontario Arts Council, Black Moss Press, Brick Books, *Descant*, *The New Quarterly* and Wolsak & Wynn, all of whom financially supported the writing at various stages.

Thanks to Alex Greer, Camilla Holland, Brian Jantzi, Sarah Rotering and Herman Silochan. Thanks also to Tina Srebotnjak, Carol Barbour, Joseph Romain, Sheina Barnes and all the staff at TPL, especially the folks at the Annette Street Branch.

"Child's Room" first appeared in *Where Babies Come From* (Tall Tree Press, 2009). The Tool Shed section was published by Gaspereau Press in 2005 as No.13 in the Devil's Whim occasional chapbook series. Thanks to Crispin and Jan Elsted, Andrew Steeves, Kate Kennedy, Don McKay and Roo Borson for their sensitive help in fulfilling the intentions of these pieces.

Glen Downie has published half a dozen books of poetry and in 2008 was awarded the Toronto Book Award for his collection, *Loyalty Management*. His work has appeared in the secondary school textbook *Inside Poetry*, as well as in many anthologies and journals. Formerly a social worker in cancer care, he served a term as writer-in-residence at Dalhousie University's Medical Humanities Program before returning to a life of anonymity in Toronto as an at-home father.